SOCIA

 @the_coach_scott

 @the_coach_scott

 @divorcerecoverycoach

 @the_coach_scott

TABLE OF CONTENTS

This book is dedicated to all of my children.
I love you very much and I hope that
I make you all proud to call me Daddy.

I'd like to thank my ex wife Amy for
10 years of marriage, 3 beautiful children,
and for divorcing me. You pushed me to
become the best man and father that
I could be. You will always have my love
and respect and I pray you find
happiness. Without you, this book
and ministry would not have happened.

Special thanks to Brandi O'Dell and Cori Jean
for helping me find my way in my healing and
in the process of writing this book and showing
up when I needed it most.

"The greatest war ever fought, and are still fighting, where more people have been defeated and died, is the war within."
— Anthony Liccione

INTRO

If you would've told me 10 years ago that my marriage would not survive, I would have looked you in the eye and told you that you were a fool. My marriage would not survive? Ha! My marriage had already survived so many things and nothing would ever make it fail. At least that was my mentality. The woman I was married to was IT for me. I was madly in love, and I had plans to be with her until the day that I died. It's funny how things change though. One minute everything is right on track and the next minute the whole train crashes into a deep valley and explodes.

My divorce came bundled as an uncontested surrender of everything that I believed in down to my core. In my mind, divorce was not an option. We were supposed to fight for our family and never give up on each other. Till death do us part. That was what I believed. As a kid I was very familiar with divorce. My mom had been married and divorced numerous times, and I always swore to myself that if I ever got married, it would be for life. So you can understand why I was so hurt and triggered when it happened to me and to my kids. I didn't want it to happen. I didn't want my kids to see or feel what I had felt when I was younger. But sometimes you must let go and let God. He has been doing this a lot longer than we have and he knows best.

After the last big argument with my wife, I distinctly remember praying to God: "if this is not what you have for us anymore, please make it abundantly clear". 2 months later he answered. Divorce happened. I stood in my shower one morning crying my eyeballs out. I was hurt and I was angry at God. I asked him "why are you allowing this to happen to my family?".

I wasn't expecting him to answer me, but he did. I heard God say "why are you so mad about me answering your prayer from 2 months ago? You said if this is not what I have for you to make it abundantly clear. So, I did". I had no idea that the year that followed would teach me more about myself than I had known for 44 years. You see it wasn't just my divorce that I had to face. I have been dealing with Post Traumatic Stress Disorder since I was 17. I had a deep-rooted fear of not being enough and being abandoned. My kids were no longer at my house every night. I lost my best friend and my wife. I was also terrified of being alone due to a heart attack 2 years before. All these fears and anxieties were dumped on me all at once and it nearly broke me. After months of depression, anxiety and lack of sleep, I had lost 27 pounds and I was a mess. But I woke up one day and looked in the mirror. Enough was enough. I was not going to live my life like I was attending a funeral any longer. Running from all my pain, doubts, and fears was not working. I could never run far enough or fast enough to get away from them. I had to face them. It was time to GO TO WAR.

In this book, you are going to see the process that I designed to help you heal and to become the best version of you, FOR YOU. Remember that nothing changes if nothing changes. It is important to pace yourself with the book. Follow the weekly battles and weekly assessments and do not rush ahead. This is a PROCESS and you need to focus on each battle, not the entire outcome of the war.

REALITY CHECK

There is a hard reality that you must accept. In 2024, 50% of all marriages end in divorce. As hard as that may be to accept, I believe there is more to the story. What about the marriages that stay together for the kids or other reasons like finances? When you add those factors in, that means that around 75% of all marriages FAIL. Other statistics say that 60% of first marriages include one person who has been married before. 65% of all second marriages and 75% of all third or more marriages end in divorce. Why is that? I believe it's because of 2 reasons. The first is that God is not the head of that relationship. The second is because we go into relationships as unhealed versions of ourselves and the damage bleeds through and ends up ruining the marriage. We are all products of our childhood.

Sadly, you are now one of those statistics. This doesn't mean that it is your fault or that you are a failure. But that does mean that you have to come to some harsh realities and truths. You are divorced. You are single. You are alone. But most of all, you are going to be ok if you do the work. You are going to have to grieve the relationship and there are 5 stages to the grieving process.

The most painful thing that you need to realize is that no one is coming to the rescue. This is all on you and it's your responsibility to do the work to heal. I'm not just talking about the pain of your divorce. You need to go back and heal those inner wounds from the past so that you can become secure in yourself. Sure, you can externalize your pain and seek a rebound relationship, start partying, shopping more, or turning to drugs and alcohol., but none of those things are going to solve the problem. You are going to have to dig deep and face things that may make you uncomfortable, sad, or anxious. This is where it may be very beneficial for you to seek some sort of therapy or counseling beyond this book. Do whatever it takes!

As you begin to fight these battles, you have to do the work. You have to show up for you. I know that a lot of you will struggle with that part because you have always shown up for everyone else, but never for yourself. It's time to focus on you and what it takes to become who you have always wanted and needed to be.

I have been exactly where you are. I know it hurts and I know that it feels like you are dying. You are not dying! You just can't remember how to live. This book is going to help you remember and it's going to help you find yourself again.

FIRST CHECK IN

MOOD

WHAT IS HURTING YOU THE MOST?

DESCRIBE YOUR STRONGEST FEELINGS

WHAT ARE YOU MOST AFRAID OF RIGHT NOW?

WHAT ARE YOU HOPING TO GAIN FROM THIS JOURNEY?

WHERE CAN YOU SEE YOURSELF 5 YEARS FROM NOW?

LET THE BATTLES BEGIN...

BATTLES FOR WEEK 1

1. GRIEVE IT

2. FEEL IT

3. NO/LOW CONTACT

4. GET OFF YOUR BUTT

2 TIMOTHY 3:1-5

3 But understand this, that in the last days there will come times of difficulty. 2 For people will be lovers of self, lovers of money, proud, arrogant, abusive, disobedient to their parents, ungrateful, unholy, 3 heartless, unappeasable, slanderous, without self-control, brutal, not loving good, 4 treacherous, reckless, swollen with conceit, lovers of pleasure rather than lovers of God, 5 having the appearance of godliness, but denying its power. **Avoid such people.**

1. GRIEVE IT

We have all experienced grief in or lives. The pain that comes with grief can seem unbearable, but you need to understand that grief is a process. Like all processes, it is going to take time for you to get through it. You don't eat the apples the same day that you plant the seeds. If you don't take time to grieve, you are going to sweep those feelings under the rug until one day you finally trip over it. Lets look at the stages of grief so you know what to expect in this war.

SHOCK

You are probably experiencing numbness in this stage. The news that someone wants a divorce or that they cheated has you in a state of disbelief and denial that this is actually happening. This is how your emotions defend themselves from the pain as a form of protecting you from being completely overwhelmed. This can last days to weeks. You may be asking "why are you doing this?" or "how did we get here?", Many people withdraw from everyone at this stage.

ANGER

Anger is one of the most helpful feelings that you will feel in the grieving process. It will be so much easier for you to see them for who they are and what they did. The question of "why are you doing this?" goes to a statement like "How dare you do this!". Being angry can also get you in trouble if you don't harness it properly. Do not do anything out of emotion. It is so easy to want to lash out and say words that you won't hear at church, but don't! The bible says "be angry but do not sin" and also to "not let the sun go down in anger so that you don't give the devil any opportunity". Ephesians 4. This stage can repeat itself as you learn new details about an affair or when you see them with someone new.

BARGAINING

During this stage, many people begin to analyze the marriage and how it ended. What could have been done better? What could have been said? You may feel deep sadness and a sense of being lost at this stage. It is normal for many people to want to reach back out to the ex and try to restore the marriage. If you were with a narcissist or in a toxic relationship, do not do this!

DEPRESSION

This is the stage that most people get stuck in. You are extremely sad and you have lost energy to go to work, clean your house, or even get out of bed. This is NORMAL! Remember that this is a grieving PROCESS. It is ok to feel these feelings. After all, you are grieving the loss of a relationship and the loss of all the plans that were made. It is very important to do the work in this book so that you don't get stuck here.

ACCEPTANCE

The purpose of this entire book is to get you to this stage. I can assure you that this stage is amazing because you feel like you are living again and you can actually move on with your life. You can accept what happened, begin to co-parent, and even seek a new relationship.

2. FEEL IT

Right now you are probably doing everything in your power to dull and ease the pain. You may be staying inside your house, avoiding friends and family, or you may even be drinking yourself to sleep. You may also be shopping, working longer hours, or seeking another relationship. These don't fix the problem. These are just band-aids. You need to accept and face the pain that you are feeling. There is a common quote that says "in order to GROW through it, you must GO through it". I saw this in my own healing journey and i can promise you that you are going to have to go through it all. I also promise you that if you do, you will grow from it.

CRY & SAY IT

Think back to when you experienced heartache in your life. Maybe this was the loss of a loved one or a breakup. Remember how hard you cried during that time and then think of how you felt after. You probably felt a lot better. I challenge you to set aside time every day to cry your eyeballs out. You need to let it all out and keep letting it out because your body and mind need to release that hurt. As the song from FROZEN says " Let it go, Let it go. Can't hold it back anymore". I also challenge you to say "I am single, I am divorced, I am alone" out loud as often as you need to. This will help in the acceptance of where you are now.

3.NO/LOW CONTACT

If I called you an addict, how would you feel? You probably wouldn't like that very much, but it could be the truth. There's a good chance that the person that you are divorcing or have divorced was a toxic person. During the time of your relationship you became addicted to the ups and downs, hot and cold, and you became *Trauma Bonded*. This is when someone made you feel so amazing in the beginning. It was everything that you wanted until it wasn't. The same person who love bombed you and promised you the world became the same person who tore you down. The problem is that you began to believe that they were the only one who could get you back to that high when y'all first got together. So, you depend on them to bring you back up just so they can tear you down again. This is not a good cycle and it must be broken just like addiction. The only solution is to detach from these people so that you can detox from these people.

NO CONTACT

This means you have to quit "cold turkey". The only way to break a trauma bond and remove these toxic people is to block them, delete them, get a restraining order, or whatever it takes to keep them away from you. They are a drug. You are addicted. Remember that every time you have contact with them, it can reset your healing clock back to zero. Keep them away and keep moving forward.

LOW CONTACT

Just because you have kids with someone doesn't mean that they have control over you. You are no longer a doormat to anyone. This is YOUR life.

Low contact is for you to set a hard boundary with your toxic ex. You will only communicate through text, email, co-parenting apps or a mediator. This is so you can keep evidence for court or child custody battles. When the conversations take place you will use 2 methods that I recommend. The first is the B.I.F.F method by Bill Eddy, and the J.A.D.E method. BIFF stands for Brief, Informative, Friendly, and Firm. In the JADE method you are not going to Justify, Argue, Defend, or Explain anything to your toxic ex. If your ex attacks, disrespects, or ridicules anything about you or your parenting , you are not going to engage. Not answering is often the best answer. They are just trying to get a reaction out of you and they will attack things that they know will trigger you. Do not take the bait. Take time to research B.I.F.F and J.A.D.E and use them every day.

4. GET OFF YOUR BUTT

One of the most therapeutic things that I began to do was going to the gym. No matter what I was feeling or how much my brain would not slow down, I could go to the gym and work it all out. You have heard the saying "idle hands are the devils playground", but I believe that an idle mind is even worse. Going to the gym allows you to release so much stress and anxiety and gives your mind something to focus on besides all the negative. I also found that going for walks every single day were extremely beneficial for my physical and mental health. When I say "walks", I'm not talking about a Sunday stroll. Remember that we are at WAR. I walk at a pace like I ate some bad Taco Bell and I need to get to a bathroom. I'm sure you know exactly what I mean. You have to walk with a purpose.

EXERCISE

Decide today that you are going to start going to a gym, running, walking, biking or any other exercise program. I don't care what you do, just start and then be consistent. DO SOMETHING! Starting today you will walk every single day of the week for at least 30 minutes. NO LESS!

PLEDGE

I,_____ pledge to to start showing up for ME. I will begin an exercise program this week and I will CONSISTENTLY show up and GO TO WAR. I owe this to myself. I understand that no one else is going to do this work for me and it is MY responsibility to become who I want to become for ME.

_____

WEEKLY CHECK IN

MOOD

THE *WORST* MOMENT

THE *BEST* MOMENT

WHAT ARE YOU *PROUD* OF THIS WEEK?

WHAT ARE YOU *THANKFUL* FOR THIS WEEK?

WHAT DO YOU WANT TO *IMPROVE* ON?

JOURNAL SPACE

FINISH THIS BATTLE BEFORE MOVING FORWARD

THE LEAKING PIPE

I want you to imagine a house. This house is the healthy, normal version of you. Inside the walls of this house is a water pipe. As we go through life, we experience pain and trauma and this causes the pipe to leak. The more you experience, the more the pipe leaks. The more the pipe leaks, the more damage it's going to cause in your house. The smart thing to do would be to fix the pipe (counseling, coaching, etc.). But we don't do that do we? We usually just ignore the leak and put up new walls and paint and call it fixed. Then, you are confused as to why the house (relationships) keeps falling apart. Until you are willing to tear down those walls and fix the leak, nothing will change. You cannot fix what you refuse to face. That leaking pipe is responsible for your *Attachment Style,* the way that you choose a partner for relationships, how you see yourself, and so much more. Are you ready to fix the leak?

We must first identify what caused the leak. This could be caused by a person, an event, or even how you received or didn't receive love as a kid. As you begin the battles for week 1, please understand that this battle may be hard for you. It may bring up a lot of old wounds. You may even experience fear and anxiety as you write. Do it anyway! This is the leaking pipe.

BATTLES FOR WEEK 2

1. FIND YOUR KNEES

2. JOURNALING

3. WHO HURT YOU?

4. NO REBOUNDS

ROMANS 10:17

So faith comes from hearing, and hearing through the word of Christ.

ROMANS 15:13

May the God of hope fill you with all joy and peace in believing, so that by the power of the Holy Spirit you may abound in hope.

1. FIND YOUR KNEES

I don't believe I would have survived what I went through if it had not been for my faith. Some of you may be angry with God right now and that's ok. That doesn't change the fact that he is still God and he is in control of everything at all times. God knows everything, hears everything, and he sees everything. I firmly believe that when we go through the pain of breakups and divorce, it is God pulling the strings. Jeremiah 29:11 tells us that he has plans for our lives. Sometimes God has to remove people, even if it hurts you, so you can get back on track with his plans for your life. It is so important to trust and have faith that God knows what he is doing. He's got this.....

SEEKING GOD

I challenge you to set aside 30 minutes of every day to study your bible and for prayer. Pray anywhere and everywhere. God loves his children and he doesn't just want weekend visitations.

Set up a war room in your house. This could be a closet or a corner of a room. Write down your prayers on sticky notes and post them to the wall. Pray for these things. When they are answered, put them in a big jar to save.

2. JOURNAL

Journaling is one of the most effective tools that you can use to heal. Some therapists recommend you journal every day or multiple times a day. Other therapists recommend that you journal once per week. I believe you should journal once per week unless you need to clear your mind or in specific situations. Some of you will be ok with once a week while others may need to journal more. I have provided space at the end of each week for you to journal and I have also provided a page for a weekly recap for you.

The reason for journaling is for you to take all those thoughts that are banging around in your brain and put them on paper. When you are stuck in your thoughts, everything is going very fast. You cannot process them all. But when you have to write them down, your brain must slow down to process the thoughts so you can put them onto paper. Remember that journaling will not help if you don't do it. I like to say that journaling is a way for us to take the trash out of our minds. Be sure to take the trash out every week.

3. WHO HURT YOU?

How long have you kept your mouth shut? All those things that you needed to say have been buried deep inside of you for way too long. You needed to tell them how you felt. They needed to know how much they hurt and scarred you. But you never spoke up. You have been carrying the weight of all that pain and trauma and now is your chance to say it!

WRITE A LETTER TO EVERY PERSON WHO HAS EVER HURT YOU.

You are not going to mail these letters. This is an opportunity to unload a lot of trash out of your mind and heart. Tell these people exactly what you have always wanted to say to them. Let it all go! DO NOT SKIP THIS BATTLE. When you complete these letters it will help you to feel better, but also identify where your pipe began to leak.

On the next page write down what thoughts and feelings you have about writing these letters and why. SAVE THE LETTERS.

4. NO REBOUNDS

When we experience heartache, and find ourselves alone, we sometimes go into panic mode and try to find a rebound relationship to fill that empty hole in us. This may help for a time, but you are very likely to end up with the exact same kind of person because you haven't healed anything. DO NOT DO THIS! Do not find a sex partner, and for the love of GOD, stay far away from dating websites! I believe that these dating sites only provide a 2% chance for you to find a compatible match anyway, and you are not ready. There is a good chance that you have never been single or alone and it's very uncomfortable. You have gone from relationship to relationship and the only thing that changed was the persons name. There is a reason behind this. You are not healed. Now is the time to stay single. Remember that the solution to your problems is not between someone else's legs or a rebound situationship.

ONE YEAR

I challenge you to stay single for ONE YEAR. Yes, ONE YEAR. I'm sure that seems like a long time, but you have been living in hell for years. Can't you take one full year for yourself? This is your apology tour to yourself. ONE YEAR!

PLEDGE

I,_____ pledge to stay single for no less that one year so that I can work on myself, and so I can become the best version of myself that I can be.

_____

WEEKLY CHECK IN

MOOD

THE WORST MOMENT

THE BEST MOMENT

WHAT ARE YOU PROUD OF THIS WEEK?

WHAT ARE YOU THANKFUL FOR THIS WEEK?

WHAT DO YOU WANT TO IMPROVE ON?

JOURNAL SPACE

FINISH THIS
BATTLE
BEFORE
MOVING
FORWARD

BATTLES FOR WEEK 3

1. LOOK IN THE MIRROR

2. STICKS & STONES

3. CONTROL THE CONTROLLABLES

PSALM 139:23

Search me, O God, and know my heart! Try me and know my thoughts.

PROVERBS 4:29

Death and life are in the power of the tongue, and those who love it will eat its fruits.

JOSHUA 1:9

Have I not commanded you? Be strong and courageous. Do not be frightened, and do not be dismayed. for the Lord your God is with you wherever you go

1. LOOK IN THE MIRROR

I coach a lot of people every week. One of the most common trends that I see in my sessions, is the fact that most people have had numerous failed relationships. Some people will even say things like "I've been married 4 times and all 4 times they were abusive" or " every person I've been with has cheated on me". My question to them is always, *"What is the common denominator in all of these relationships?"*. It's you! We all carry wounds and scars from our childhood. How we were loved or not loved when we were younger plays a major roll in how we see ourselves in adulthood and in relationships. So I want to encourage you to go and look in the mirror. No, seriously, GO LOOK IN THE MIRROR! The person that you see in the reflection is who you are going to *go to war* with. You are responsible for your own healing.

WHAT DO YOU SEE?

On a separate piece of paper, be honest with what you see in the mirror. What do you hate about yourself? What negative beliefs do you have of yourself? SAVE THIS PAPER.

WHILE YOU'RE THERE

Since you are already looking in the mirror, I want to challenge you. In the space below, write down all the things that you wish people would tell you, or things you have always needed to hear (I.E. you are worthy, you are loved, you are enough, etc.).

STICKY NOTES

Now that you know what you wish people would say to you, I want you to write them all down on sticky notes. Stick them to the mirror in your bathroom, the refrigerator, your car dash, or wherever you will see them every day. Once you have done this, these are the things you are going to say out loud to yourself every day. These are called your *Daily Affirmations*.

Daily affirmations are a very valuable way to change the channel of your negative thought processes. All of the negative things that you said in the beginning of this battle are now being replaced with a positive mindset. Soon you will start to be your own cheerleader and your mindset will change.

2. STICKS & STONES

"Sticks and stone may break my bones, but words will never hurt me". Whoever came up with that statement had obviously never been through any trauma. Words can absolutely hurt. They can even break you. Most of our negative thoughts about ourselves have come from the mouths of other people. If you were with a narcissist, you know for a fact that words can hurt and they can control you. The bible says that the power of life and death is in the tongue (Proverbs 18:21). Some of the words that we have heard have killed us on the inside. We lose confidence, self esteem, self worth, and we also feel shame. This is why most of you listed a lot of negative things about yourself in Battle #1. Now its time to make a different list.

MAKE A LIST

On a separate piece of paper, I want you to list as many mean and hurtful things that people have said to you or done to you. SAVE THE LIST.

On the next page, explain how all of these things make you feel. Why?

3. CONTROL THE CONTROLLABLES

You may be in a situation where it feels like you have no power over what is happening. It could be a situation like:

- You can't see your kids
- You got kicked out of the house
- Your ex has a new person around your kids
- They are telling lies about you to everyone
- Maybe it's the divorce itself

Some of these situations can be handled in the court system, and some of them cannot be controlled at all. You have got to focus on the things you CAN control. How you REACT is a good example of what is controllable. You can't control what people do or say, but you can control how you react to these situations.

I get it. They are telling lies about you and you want to defend yourself or maybe take off your shoes, pull some hair and throw some punches. That won't solve any problems. It will create more and make you look like the monster they are making you out to be. Exodus 14:14 tells us that *God will fight your battles for you, and you have only to be SILENT.* Did you catch that? GOD will FIGHT the battles FOR you and all you need to do is SHUT UP!

CAN YOU CONTROL IT

Write down every problem you are facing. Then write down what you CAN and CANNOT control about each one. Be realistic

Any problem that you cannot control, STOP FOCUSING ON IT and GIVE IT TO GOD.

Use this for any future situations you may encounter.

WEEKLY CHECK IN

MOOD

THE WORST MOMENT

THE BEST MOMENT

WHAT ARE YOU PROUD OF THIS WEEK?

WHAT ARE YOU THANKFUL FOR THIS WEEK?

WHAT DO YOU WANT TO IMPROVE ON?

JOURNAL SPACE

FINISH THIS
BATTLE
BEFORE
MOVING
FORWARD

NEW CONTACT

I bet you still have your ex saved as "my baby" or something sweet or sentimental. When you are in the healing process, one of the most helpful things you can do is to update their contact information. Instead of those sweet and cute names that you have for them, it's time to change their name to what is real. If your ex was toxic, abusive or a narcissist, I want to challenge you to store them as something different. Take the name of your ex then add some reality to it. The new contact will look something like this:

- Jason- He didn't care
- Christy- The liar
- Matthew- The narc
- Stephanie- Stay no contact
- Ashley- Do not engage

Every time you get a call or text from them, you will be reminded of who they actually are and what they did.

BATTLES FOR WEEK 4

1. BURN IT

2. FORGIVE

3. CHANGE THE CHANNEL

ISAIAH 48:10

Behold, I have refined you, but not as silver; I have tried you in the furnace of affliction.

MATTHEW 6:13-14

For if you forgive others their trespasses, your heavenly Father will also forgive you, but if you do not forgive others their trespasses, neither will your Father forgive your trespasses.

1. BURN IT

For months after my divorce, I continued to save so many things from my marriage. I had all the canvas pictures of our family and gifts that I had received for anniversaries stored in my closet attached to the hope that my wife would come back. As I began my healing journey, I knew that something had to change. I could not keep going forward while I was still looking back. The decision was made to take everything that I was saving, stack it all up in my back yard, and burn it all. Yes, this was a little drastic, but as I watched those flames cremate the last remains of my marriage, I felt at peace. I felt like a Viking burning his ships because there was no going back. My war had begun.

CREMATION

If there is anything that you are holding onto in hopes of reconciliation that is not tied up in the divorce (Don't Do Anything Illegal), stack it up in a fireplace or in the yard outside. But here is the awesome part....

As you are preparing to have one final funeral for your marriage, go get the letters from Week 2 and the lists from Week 3. YOU NEED TO HAVE A FUNERAL FOR ALL OF THAT TOO! Burn the letters to those who hurt you! Burn the list of all the mean and hurtful things! Burn the negative things you saw in the mirror! CREMATE IT and lets move on with your life.

2. FORGIVE

Now that you have had a funeral for your marriage and for the pain and negativity of your past, it is time to find some peace. I found that forgiving everyone from my past who had hurt me, abandoned me, betrayed me, and ridiculed me, took a huge weight off my shoulders. We were not meant to carry those loads. That is where God comes in. He can carry all of the weight of it and he can carry you.

Please understand that FORGIVENESS does not mean that you are APPROVING of what they did or said. You are forgiving them FOR YOU.

"Forgive others, not because they deserve forgiveness, but because you deserve peace."
- Jonathan Huie

FORGIVE THEM LETTERS

Write another short letter to those people again. But this time I want you to say "I forgive you for…", and fill in the rest of the details. On the next page, I challenge you to write yourself a letter of forgiveness too.

3. CHANGE THE CHANNEL

Rumination is defined as *the action or process of thinking deeply about something*. How much time have you spent thinking about your situation? Why did they cheat? How many times? Are they missing me? How could they do this? What went wrong? Am I going to die alone? Who will want me now? These are things that you are probably spending way too much time thinking about. It is ok to feel these feelings and think these thoughts, but we don't want to get STUCK there. When we get stuck in overthinking or feeling negative, I call that CHANNEL ONE. That channel is noisy, full of static, and it's not even in color. CHANNEL ONE SUCKS! Change the channel!

CHANGE THE CHANNEL

Anytime you find yourself stuck in rumination, do 20 squats, go for a walk or run, call a friend or family member, or do anything to change that channel.

WEEKLY CHECK IN

MOOD

THE WORST MOMENT

THE BEST MOMENT

WHAT ARE YOU PROUD OF THIS WEEK?

WHAT ARE YOU THANKFUL FOR THIS WEEK?

WHAT DO YOU WANT TO IMPROVE ON?

JOURNAL SPACE

FINISH THIS BATTLE BEFORE MOVING FORWARD

Look at you! You have survived your first month of No/Low Contact and of your healing journey. It is ok to pause during this journey, but make sure that even if you stumble, GET BACK UP and start again.

Let me remind you that THIS IS A PROCESS. You are going to have good days and bad days. Keep going. You've got this.

Coach Scott

BATTLES FOR WEEK 5

1. SELF LOVE

2. GET SUPPORT

EPHESIANS 5:29

For no one ever hated his own flesh, but nourishes and cherishes it, just as Christ does the church,

ECCLESIASTES 4:9-12

Two are better than one, because they have a good reward for their toil. For if they fall, one will lift up his fellow. But woe to him who is alone when he falls and has not another to lift him up! Again, if two lie together, they keep warm, but how can one keep warm alone? And though a man might prevail against one who is alone, two will withstand him a threefold cord is not quickly broken.

1. SELF LOVE

Many of you have a hard time loving anything about yourself and SELF LOVE is a phrase that may be non-existent in your vocabulary. Most of the people that I coach lack love for THEMSELVES. This is one of the reasons that people end up in toxic relationships. When you don't love yourself, you become dependent on other people to love you. The problem with this is if the relationship fails, you won't have that love anymore and you will feel empty again and again.

When you start to prioritize yourself over others, it may make you uncomfortable. That is probably because you have always put everyone else first. Putting everyone else first drains you of so much energy and leaves you with nothing left in the tanks especially when you don't even get the bare minimum in return. It's time to start loving YOU and taking care of YOU.

LOVE YOU

I challenge you to start doing things to love on yourself. Some of examples of this are:

- Routinely get your hair cut or colored
- Get a makeover
- Take yourself shopping
- Get a massage
- Start a skin care routine
- Buy something you have always wanted
- Listen to music
- Remove negative people from your life
- Turn off your phone

2. GET SUPPORT

The bible tells a story of a man who was paralyzed and how his friends were trying to get him in to see Jesus so that he could be healed. Unfortunately the friends could not get the man into the house where Jesus was, so they removed a section of the roof and lowered the paralyzed man down to Jesus. Jesus then healed this man. The moral of this story is that YOUR FRIENDS MATTER. During this time of healing it is important to surround yourself with people who would take the roof off of a house to help you. Hopefully you have friends who are trying to get you closer to Jesus also.

You need to understand that there are millions of people who are going through or have gone through your situation. Surrounding yourself with these people is one of the best healing steps that you can do.

SURROUND YOURSELF

I challenge you to get involved with Facebook groups or local groups that are for people who have gone through similar things and become a part of these groups. Be sure to participate actively in the discussions.

facebook.com/gotowargroup

WEEKLY CHECK IN

MOOD

THE *WORST* MOMENT

THE *BEST* MOMENT

WHAT ARE YOU *PROUD* OF THIS WEEK?

WHAT ARE YOU *THANKFUL* FOR THIS WEEK?

WHAT DO YOU WANT TO *IMPROVE* ON?

JOURNAL SPACE

FINISH THIS BATTLE BEFORE MOVING FORWARD

BATTLES FOR WEEK 6

1. MAKE 2 LISTS

2. BREAK SOMETHING

LUKE 12:6-7
Are not five sparrows sold for two pennies? And not one of them is forgotten before God. Why, even the hairs of your head are all numbered. Fear not, you are of more value than many sparrows.

PSALMS 31:24
Be strong and let your heart take courage, all you who wait for the Lord!

1. MAKE 2 LISTS

One of the most helpful things that I did in my healing process was to make 2 lists. These lists opened my eyes to reality and helped me let go of the fantasy of my marriage. Once the fantasy is gone and you take them off of the pedestal you have had them on, you can finally see the truth. Follow the steps below:

"If You don't know your own value, someone will tell you your value, and it'll be less than you're worth"

Bernard Hopkins

LIST #1

On the next page write down all of the things that you bring to the table. What things did you do right in your relationship? What do you have to offer? What are some of your best qualities?

LIST #2

On the second page write down all of the things that you could not stand about your ex. What did you actually lose? How did they treat you? Would you want your children to be married to someone like your ex?

LIST #1

LIST #2

2. BREAK SOMETHING

Has this whole process of divorce and the reasons why it happened made you angry? Do you wish that you could just throat punch someone or tell all of their dark secrets on social media? As fun as that sounds, it will not solve the problem and it will make you look like the bad person. Yet, you still carry the stress, anger, and hurt of all that you have gone through. Our bodies are like a Coke bottle that has been shaken up. The more things we face, the more it is shaken. The more it is shaken, the more it needs to let off some pressure. That is exactly what you need to do so that you don't explode!! Feel free to do any or all of the exercises below:

CHOP A LOG

Buy or borrow an axe. Then, find a log or an old tree that you can unleash all your pain and anger upon. Every time you take a swing at it, scream out something you are mad or hurt about. Do this as often as you need to now and in the future.

BREAK SOME GLASS

Breaking an old glass or plate against a brick wall or concrete feels amazing. DO IT! Every time you throw a dish or glass be sure to scream out what you are mad or hurt about. Don't forget to clean your mess up lol.

HOME RUN

Smacking something with a baseball bat has the same gratification. If you want to go to a batting cage, do so. I personally like the idea of taking a bat to an old printer, tv, gaming system or even an old car. Bust it up and try to hit a home run. Don't forget to scream out what you are mad or hurt about. Batter up! Rage rooms are also a good choice.

PEW PEW

If you are a proud 2nd amendment person, take your guns out to the range and blow some things to pieces. Again, scream out what you are mad or hurt about and send it down range

WEEKLY CHECK IN

MOOD

THE WORST MOMENT

THE BEST MOMENT

WHAT ARE YOU PROUD OF THIS WEEK?

WHAT ARE YOU THANKFUL FOR THIS WEEK?

WHAT DO YOU WANT TO IMPROVE ON?

JOURNAL SPACE

**FINISH THIS
BATTLE
BEFORE
MOVING
FORWARD**

THE HEALING CLOCK

Detaching from someone that you were addicted to is not easy. You think about the good times and how you wish things would have been different. Maybe you are still ruminating over the hopes and dreams of what you thought your marriage was supposed to be. Did you know that you can actually experience the same symptoms as someone who is detoxing from heavy narcotics? After all, they were your drug. As you work through this book, please remember that no/low contact is very important in this healing rehab. Anytime you have a conversation, especially a good conversation, you are resetting your healing clock back to ZERO! That means you have to start all over again. This can and most likely will happen to many of you. Don't give up. Get back on your feet, dust yourself off, wipe those tears, and let's get back to the battles

BATTLES FOR WEEK 7

1. ATTACHMENT STYLES

2. BOUNDARIES

MICAH 7:11
A day for the building of your walls! In that day the boundary shall be far extended.

TITUS 3:10
As for a person who stirs up division, after warning him once and then twice, have nothing more to do with him

MATTHEW 11:28
Come to me, all who labor and are heavy laden, and I will give you rest.

1. ATTACHMENT STYLES

When I first learned about attachment styles, it was like I was introduced to myself for the first time. All of the decisions that I had made with relationships and friendships finally made sense. Do you pull away during arguments or conflict? Do you sabotage your relationships when things are going too good? Are you a people pleaser who puts everyone else's needs before your own? Do you have abandonment issues? These are questions that can reveal our attachment styles.

Attachment styles are usually formed in the first 18 months of a child's life. Have you ever dropped you kid off at daycare or school and seen the child that is screaming and clinging to their parent? What about the kid that walks in, kisses their mom, then runs off to play with no problem? The first kid has a fear that their parent will not return. That is what anxious attachment can look like. The second kid KNOWS his parent will come back, so they can go play with no fear.

Mary Ainsworth, a Psychologist in the 1970's, did a study called *the strange situation*. I highly recommend you go read that study. I also encourage you to read a book called *Attached* by Amir Levine and Rachel S.F Heller.

2. BOUNDARIES

Do you lock your car doors when you go into a store? Do you lock the doors at your home before you go to bed? Why? It's for protection right? You want to protect the things and the people that are in your life. Locked doors are a form of boundaries. Without these locked doors, people could get into your home or car and do whatever they wanted. We all need healthy boundaries in our personal lives as well. I'm sure you have figured out by now that the world is full of people who are givers and people who are takers. Takers have no regard for anyone's boundaries. Givers have no boundaries in the first place. Having boundaries can be as simple as saying "no" or "I'm not going to do that". Below, I am going to give you a reading assignment. The books that are listed have helped me to learn why boundaries need to be implemented and how to enforce them. Take the time to read these books as you continue to grow and heal.

- *Boundaries* by Henry Cloud
- *Healthy Boundaries* by Chase Hill

WEEKLY CHECK IN

MOOD

THE WORST MOMENT

THE BEST MOMENT

WHAT ARE YOU PROUD OF THIS WEEK?

WHAT ARE YOU THANKFUL FOR THIS WEEK?

WHAT DO YOU WANT TO IMPROVE ON?

JOURNAL SPACE

FINISH THIS BATTLE BEFORE MOVING FORWARD

BATTLES FOR WEEK 8

1. BE A KID AGAIN

2. CREATE NEW ROUTINES

3. GET GROUNDED

PROVERBS 3:5-6

Trust in the Lord with all your heart, and do not lean on your own understanding. In all your ways acknowledge him, and he will make straight your paths.

PSALM 34:4

I sought the Lord, and he answered me and delivered me from all my fears.

1. BE A KID AGAIN

Think back to a time when you were a kid. Do you remember all the fun things you used to do that would make time stand still? For me, it was bass fishing. No matter what I was feeling or facing, I could always go bass fishing and the world would fade away. Walking the beach is another thing that takes me back to my childhood. The smell of the ocean and the sand on my feet have always given me peace. For you, it may have been staring at the stars, coloring in coloring books, watching movies, riding bikes, or swimming. These are the things that you need to return to.

BE CHILDISH

On the following page I challenge you to write down as many things that you loved to do as a kid. Once you have this list, start doing them again. Have fun!

2. CREATE NEW ROUTINES

We are all creatures of habits. Some of these are good habits and some are bad habits. As we begin to set certain routines in our lives, a lot of things happen. Routines benefit us by:

- Reducing Stress
- Giving us a purpose
- Improving our mental health
- Having structure
- Achieving goals
- Helping us improve our sleep patterns
- & more

MAKE YOUR BED

I challenge you to make your bed first thing in the morning. This give you your first win of the day and can help set the tone of how the day will be.

READ

I challenge you to take 15 minutes each day to read some sort of self improvement book or study your bible.

EXERCISE

I challenge you to set an alarm and start your day off with exercise. I prefer mornings because it releases dopamine into your body and puts you in a good mood for the day.

GO TO BED

I challenge you to go to bed consistently at the same time every night. After all, sleep is one of the most important things we can do for our physical and mental health. Be sure to sleep in complete darkness.

What routines will you implement?

3. GET GROUNDED

Think back to a time when you visited a beach or walked barefoot outside. Remember how amazing the sand felt on your toes, and how just being at the beach or outside with no shoes, made you feel happy and relaxed. There is a scientific reason for this. Our bodies store electricity as we move throughout the day and with all of the electrical devices that we are around. This electrical charge can cause negative effects on our bodies. By grounding we can reduce inflammation, make our blood thinner, heal wounds faster, help your sleep issues, and can even help your mental and emotional help.

TAKE OFF YOUR SHOES

I challenge you to take 15-30 minutes each day and walk barefoot on the ground. This can be your lawn, a dirt road, the beach, a shoreline, or anywhere else that you can touch the earth barefooted.

WEEKLY CHECK IN

THE WORST MOMENT

MOOD

THE BEST MOMENT

WHAT ARE YOU PROUD OF THIS WEEK?

WHAT ARE YOU THANKFUL FOR THIS WEEK?

WHAT DO YOU WANT TO IMPROVE ON?

JOURNAL SPACE

FINISH THIS BATTLE BEFORE MOVING FORWARD

You have now completed TWO MONTHS of no/low contact and healing work! I am so proud of you! How does it feel? Are you still doing good? Are you still being consistent or have you broken your contact rules with your ex? If so, it is ok. Get back up and keep moving forward! Don't you dare quit!

Remember, THIS IS A PROCESS. You are going to have good days and bad days. Keep going. You've got this.

Coach Scott

BATTLES FOR WEEK 9

1. PASSIONS

2. COMFORT ZONE

1 PETER 4:10

As each has received a gift, use it to serve one another, as good stewards of God's varied grace.

HEBREWS 10:24-25

And let us consider how to stir up one another to love and good works, not neglecting to meet together, as is the habit of some, but encouraging one another, and the more as you see the Day drawing near.

1. PASSIONS

If you could do 3 things that bring you peace and joy, what would they be? These are things that you are passionate about and that give you purpose. When we have a passion that we never pursue, we end up with regrets later in life. Do these things! Have no regrets! You deserve to have joy and peace in your life and you deserve to be able to do the things that you are passionate about. I believe you should chase these passions because they may be gifts that God has given you for his purpose. Use them to honor him.

INVEST IN YOUR PASSIONS

If you like fishing, get the tools to fish with. If you like painting, buy the tools to paint with. If you like to do makeup, buy the brushes, take the classes, learn new techniques. No matter what your passions may be. INVEST IN THEM. This will help you to discover purpose, relieve stress and anxiety, and will give you motivation.

2. COMFORT ZONE

Imagine living your life on repeat every single day. You wake up, get ready for work, struggle out of the door and head to a job that you cannot stand. Then you get home, cook or grab dinner from town, take a shower and get ready for bed. The morning comes and the cycle repeats. Remember when you challenged new routines in Battle 2 of Week 8? You need to break this cycle. Too often we are afraid of doing anything that challenges our comfort zone. I am a huge advocate of pushing the limits of that.....

I challenge you to try any or all of the ideas below or come up with your own. Step out!

LEARN TO DANCE

Take a line dancing or hip hop dance class. Learn to do the tango or take salsa lessons. The choice is yours but STEP OUT!

TAP OUT

If you are someone who struggles with boundaries or someone who lacks confidence, i HIGHLY recommend you take Jiu Jitsu, kick boxing, or MMA classes. Many of my female clients have started these classes and they love them.

DATE YOURSELF

I challenge you to take yourself on a date. Go to the local bar and grill, sit at the bar and order your food. Be sure to dress up like you are going on a date.

SCUBA DIVING

Find a local place that teaches scuba diving classes and sign up asap. Imagine all the places you could have fun with this new skill

JUMP

Find a local place that teaches skydiving or bunjee jumping. I don't think I need to explain how much of a comfort zone you would step out of with either of these choices.

MOVIES

Find a movie in theatres that you want to go see. Buy the popcorn, get the skittles and a drink, and enjoy the movie alone.

GO FOR A DRIVE

Get in your vehicle, roll the windows down, and turn the music up. Go for an hour long ride to anywhere that you can enjoy the wind, the scenery, the music, and the peace.

WEEKLY CHECK IN

MOOD

THE WORST MOMENT

THE BEST MOMENT

WHAT ARE YOU PROUD OF THIS WEEK?

WHAT ARE YOU THANKFUL FOR THIS WEEK?

WHAT DO YOU WANT TO IMPROVE ON?

JOURNAL SPACE

FINISH THIS BATTLE BEFORE MOVING FORWARD

THE EASY BUTTON

Nearly everyone that I coach is looking for one thing: The EASY BUTTON. This is the button that makes all the pain go away. This is also the button that helps you skip all of the deep work and makes your healing process go very fast. I am here to tell you that there is no easy button. There is no magic pill or perfect coaching program. There is only you, the pain, and the process. Stop looking for a quick way to fix this. Do the work!

BATTLES FOR WEEK 10

1. SOLO ADVENTURE

2. BE OF SERVICE

PSALM 37:4
Delight yourself in the Lord, and he will give yu the desires of your heart.

GALATIONS 5:13
For you were called to freedom, brothers. Only do not use your freedom as an opportunity for the flesh, but through love serve one another.

1. SOLO ADVENTURE

Most of the clients that I coach have one thing in common: They are absolutely bothered by the thought of being ALONE. I always ask them "what is the worst thing that can happen if you are alone?". Is a rabid vampire dragon going to climb through the roof and eat you? No. Is your head going to explode into a million pieces? No. It may feel like it is, but it won't. You see, if being alone is your fear, that's exactly what you need to do. It is no different than a kid who is terrified of the water. His mom takes him out into the edge of the ocean and he immediately panics, grabs onto his mother and screams. In his mind, this is the end, and he is going to die. He doesn't understand that he is panicking over 4 inches of water. To him, it may as well be 4 miles deep. All he has to do is put his feet down and he will realize that his biggest fear is now something to laugh about and he can enjoy the very thing he was afraid of most.

The more things that you learn to do by yourself, the more you will become ok with being alone. I challenged myself to sleep in my house, alone, in silence for weeks. It definitely helps.

GO SOLO

On the next page you will find a list of ideas for you to do as a solo adventure. I challenge you to do these things.

- *Take yourself to a fancy dinner*
- *Explore your city like a tourist*
- *Go kayaking*
- *Enjoy a museum*
- *Visit the local farmers market*
- *Go for a hike*
- *Take a daytrip*
- *Go sit in the local coffee shop*
- *Ride a bike*
- *Visit a local monument or historic site*
- *Take an art class*
- *Begin music lessons*
- *Sit on the beach*
- *Start a DIY project*
- *Go camping*
- *Ride some rollercoasters*
- *Book a photoshoot*

These are just a few ideas. The sky is the limit but make sure you do these things ALONE.

2. BE OF SERVICE

The heart of a volunteer is one of the strongest things on earth. When we volunteer our time and energy to help others, it gives us purpose. It teaches us to be thankful for what we DO have in our lives instead of focusing on what we DO NOT have. Volunteering also soothes the soul, increases our mood, and our self-esteem.

Whoever brings blessing will be enriched, and one who waters will himself be watered.
Proverbs 11:25

Below are a few ideas as to where you can volunteer your time and energy and be of service:

GREATEST GENERATION

Think of an elderly person who is alone. Spend time with them, cook for them, cut their grass, or whatever else you can do to bless them.

CHURCH

Check with your local church about volunteer opportunities. They usually have plenty.

ANIMAL SHELTER

Animal shelters over very overpopulated and are always needing helpers. You may end up with a new friend lol.

COMMUNITY CLEANUP

Go to the local park, neighborhood or schools, and cleanup all the trash off the ground.

FUNDRAISERS

Start a local fundraiser to help local kids, rec departments or other organizations by doing cake walks, raffles, etc.

WEEKLY CHECK IN

MOOD

THE *WORST* MOMENT

THE *BEST* MOMENT

WHAT ARE YOU *PROUD* OF THIS WEEK?

WHAT ARE YOU *THANKFUL* FOR THIS WEEK?

WHAT DO YOU WANT TO *IMPROVE* ON?

JOURNAL SPACE

FINISH THIS BATTLE BEFORE MOVING FORWARD

BATTLES FOR WEEK 11

1. NEW HOBBY

2. SUPER MOM SUPER DAD

PSALM 127:3
Children are a heritage from the Lord, the fruit of the womb a reward.

ROMANS 8:31
What shall we say to these things? If God is for us, who can be against us?

1. NEW HOBBY

When is the last time that you tried a new hobby? I bet it has been many years because you probably "don't have time". It is time to make time. Having a hobby is an awesome way to challenge yourself and to grow as a person. Hobbies keep you engaged and work well for your mental health. One of my favorite aspects of a hobby is that it introduces you to like minded people. When you meet people with the same interests, you have now increased your support group and your circle. Did you know that being a hobbyist also relieves stress and helps to occupy your free time with fun.

"Hobbies are great distractions from the worries and troubles that plague daily living"
Bill Malone

HOBBY IDEAS

On the next page, make a list of all the hobby ideas that you would be interested in. These can be: photography, bird watching, starting a collection, gardening, and more. The choice is yours. Have fun

2. SUPER MOM/ SUPER DAD

Think back to when you were a small kid, or maybe think of a situation with your own kids. Remember when you thought your parent was super human because they could lift something heavier than you or could fix your broken toy? You may have seen this with your own kids also. My son watched me lift 190 pounds one day at the gym and said "omg Daddy, you are so strong". You see, they watch us. They look up to us. What they see from us sets the tone for who they do or don't want to become. When divorce happens and there are children involved, it makes everything harder. But, they are watching everything you do and everything you don't do. They are also listening to everything you say or don't say. The kids do not want to be caught in the middle of this mess. My question to you is this: How can you become the BEST version of mom or dad that you can be in all of this? What changes can you make to include your kids more? How can you spend more time with them? When I shifted my attention from my ex-wife to my children, it helped me focus on what I needed to do and who I needed to become. I challenge you to do the same. On the following page is a list of activities that I highly encourage you to start doing with your kids even if they are grown. You can come up with your own ideas but be consistent. Keep in mind that in some divorces, the other parent is making you out to be a monster and a bad person. Show them the opposite!

FAMILY DINNER

Once a week, setup a family dinner night. Do it every week. This would go really good with family game night

CAMPING

Going camping is one of the most awesome things that you can do with your kids. It takes them outdoors and gets them off all the electronics.

GAME NIGHT

Once a week, have a family game night. Make this a new tradition that they will remember forever.

MOVIE NIGHT

Once a week, have a family movie night. Rotate who gets to pick

NERF WAR

Buy some nerf guns and start a war with your kids. You can even surprise them by having the guns at the door when they come to visit or get home from school. Leave a note that says " Arm yourselves and prepare for battle. I am somewhere in the house, come find me".

WEEKLY CHECK IN

THE *WORST* MOMENT

MOOD

THE *BEST* MOMENT

WHAT ARE YOU *PROUD* OF THIS WEEK?

WHAT ARE YOU *THANKFUL* FOR THIS WEEK?

WHAT DO YOU WANT TO *IMPROVE* ON?

JOURNAL SPACE

FINISH THIS
BATTLE
BEFORE
MOVING
FORWARD

BATTLES FOR WEEK 12

1. TAKE THE TRIP

JEREMIAH 29:11

For I know the plans I have for you, declares the Lord, plans for welfare and not for evil, to give you a future and a hope

EXODUS 14:14

The Lord will fight for you. and you have only to be silent.

1. TAKE THE TRIP

We all have those places that we have always wanted to visit. Some of my clients have always wanted to go to France, Germany, Ireland or Greece. Others have just wanted to see Montana or The Bahamas. Planning a trip does not have to be a huge undertaking with loads of money.

One of my clients has always wanted to go to the desert and do some "overlanding". This is where off road vehicles, with camping equipment attached, travel to an area and camp. On these excursions, the trip IS the destination. Another client has always wanted to take her horses and go to the mid-west to sleep under the stars like our ancestors did in the 1800's. What ideas do you have for a trip?

PLAN A TRIP

As your final step of this program, I challenge you to plan an amazing trip to anywhere on this planet. This location has got to be somewhere that YOU have always wanted to go. It is ok to take friends and family but make sure it is YOUR destination. There's a catch though. Plans without a timeframe are just hopes and dreams. Plan it. Give it a deadline. Book it. Go!!

FINAL CHECK IN

MOOD

THE WORST MOMENT OF THIS JOURNEY

THE BEST MOMENT OF THIS JOURNEY

WHAT HAVE YOU LEARNED ABOUT YOURSELF?

HOW DO YOU FEEL NOW?

WHAT DO YOU WANT TO IMPROVE ON FOR THE FUTURE?

JOURNAL SPACE

CLOSING

My prayer for this book, and for each and every one of you, is that the words and battles have helped you to heal and to find your self-worth. You have begun to fight and to show up for yourself. But, you must continue this process as you navigate the future. This book was not the answer to all of the problems that you have faced, are facing, or will face, but I pray that it has you pointed in the right direction. If you take what I have given you in these pages, and apply them for the future, you will continue to grow and heal even more.

Remember, this is all on you, and it is YOUR responsibility to keep going forward. Set boundaries. Seek therapy or coaching. Stay in the gym. Write in your journal. Keep God first in everything. GO TO WAR!

25386690R00071